ANCIENT OSTIA

PAST AND PRESENT

According to literary tradition, the city of Ostia was founded by king Ancus Marcius at the end of the 7th century BC in an area occupied in the 8th century BC by the settlement of Ficana (today's Monte Cugno).

The oldest structures brought to light during archaeological excavations, mostly carried out between the mid-19th century and the 1940s, may, however, be dated to the early 4th century BC and it is hypothesized that they were built after the conquest of Veii, an important Etruscan center, in 396 BC. The excavations have, however, also brought to light some elements referring to a more ancient phase: fragments of architectural decoration and pottery from the 5th century and traces of huts.

Furthermore, the site of Ostia is mentioned in historic sources at least twice in connection to episodes that occurred in the 5th century BC.

View of the Charioteers street

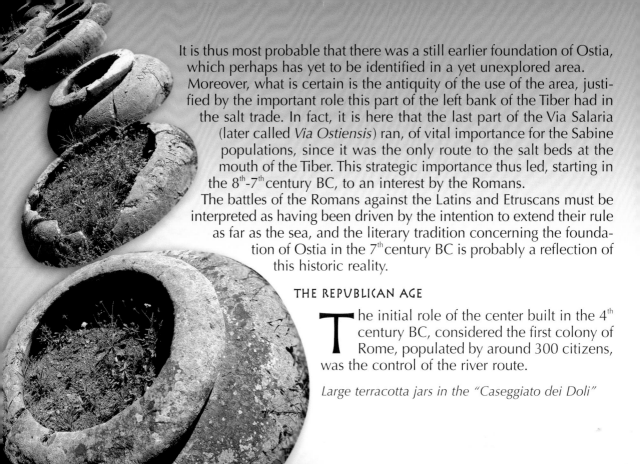

It is thus most probable that there was a still earlier foundation of Ostia, which perhaps has yet to be identified in a yet unexplored area. Moreover, what is certain is the antiquity of the use of the area, justified by the important role this part of the left bank of the Tiber had in the salt trade. In fact, it is here that the last part of the Via Salaria (later called *Via Ostiensis*) ran, of vital importance for the Sabine populations, since it was the only route to the salt beds at the mouth of the Tiber. This strategic importance thus led, starting in the 8th-7th century BC, to an interest by the Romans.

The battles of the Romans against the Latins and Etruscans must be interpreted as having been driven by the intention to extend their rule as far as the sea, and the literary tradition concerning the foundation of Ostia in the 7th century BC is probably a reflection of this historic reality.

THE REPUBLICAN AGE

The initial role of the center built in the 4th century BC, considered the first colony of Rome, populated by around 300 citizens, was the control of the river route.

Large terracotta jars in the "Caseggiato dei Doli"

The very form of the settlement, a rectangle protected by defense walls in large tuff blocks recalling those of a *castrum* (encampment), reveals its essentially military purpose.

In 267 BC the port of the colony became the headquarters of one of the commanders of the Roman fleet (the *quaestores classici*), in charge of commanding the most demanding military operations. But from 212 BC it was in the river port of Ostia that the grain intended for the military structures was stored and, progressively, the trade function prevailed over the military function. For example, the citizens of Ostia were exonerated, until 191 BC, from military service so they could devote themselves to the harbor activities, and from the end of the 2nd century BC the quaestor of Ostia mainly dealt with the importing of grain, which was to be redistributed in Rome. On the other hand, the port of Misenum on the Tyrrhenian Sea and that of Ravenna on the Adriatic became more important from the strategic standpoint. Precisely for this reason, in 87 BC, during the civil war, Marius, fighting against Sulla, who was supported by Ostia, attacked the city, which was defended only by the cavalry.

Shield, sword and helmet of a roman legionaire (Rome, Museo della Civiltà Romana)

In fact the inhabited area had grown, down through the centuries, well beyond the *castrum* walls, and only after this attack a new defense structure, of a vaster size and protected by towers, was constructed. In 67 BC the city was attacked by pirates from the East and, during the period of the 2nd triumvirate, it suffered attacks by Sextus Pompey, who was defeated only in 36 BC.

Toward the mid-1st century BC, Ostia won a greater autonomy from Rome, freeing itself from the tight control held up to that time by the quaestor, who resided there, and by several urban magistrates sent directly from Rome.

The new legislation envisaged the creation of a college of one hundred *decuriones,* with legislative power; two *duoviri,* with judicial functions, and two *aediles,* in charge of the markets and public services.

Greengrocer's funerary relief (Museum of Ostia)

To these were added, during the imperial age, two local *quaestores*, in charge of the *aerarium* (the city treasury). The highest religious office was the *pontifex Volcani*, who supervised the cult of Vulcan, the protector of the colony; after the death of Augustus, the first emperor, the office of *flamen Romae et Augusti*, in charge of the cult of the deified dead emperor, was also created.

THE IMPERIAL AGE

The commercial centrality of the port of Ostia gradually led to the need for a new harbor basin: the landing place on the river had become insufficient and was easily subject to silting; it also had only one wharf. This way, the larger ships were forced to transfer their cargo onto smaller ones, which were drawn to Rome by oxen. The problem of getting supplies to the capital could not be solved even with the aid of

Relief with warship
(Pio- Clementino Museum, Vatican)

the port of Pozzuoli, which was too far away and hard to reach, especially in the wintertime.

It was the Emperor Claudius (41-54 AD) who launched, challenging the opinion of part of the Senate, the construction of a big new facility. The intention was to construct a basin 3 km north of the mouth of the Tiber, partly dug into the mainland, and partly stretching toward the open sea with two long "pincer"-shaped wharves.

In the sea, between the wharfs, there was the large lighthouse erected on the ship built by the Emperor Caligula (37-41 AD) to transport an obelisk to the Vatican Circus (today in St. Peter's Square).

Piazzale delle Corporazioni, mosaic floor with lighthouse of the Claudian port and merchant ship

A series of canals flowing from the Tiber into the sea completed the magnificent plan. The new basin, however, revealed its lack of reliability even before its inauguration, celebrated by Nero in 64 AD with the minting of commemorative coins: in 62 AD around 200 boats were destroyed or damaged by a storm and around 100 ships, seeking shelter further up the Tiber, were struck by a devastating fire.

Fewer than 50 years later the Emperor Trajan (98-117 AD) created a new basin, with an innovative hexagonal shape, set back from the coast compared to Claudius's harbor, which probably remained active as a roadstead.

The remains of the two basins can still be seen inside the Torlonia Estate at Fiumicino. At the same time as the new constructions, the office of "food administration procurator", the magistrate in charge of food distribution, was established in Ostia.

Portrait of emperor Nero
(Rome, National Museum)

Coin of Neronian age (54-68 AD)
with the image of the port of Ostia

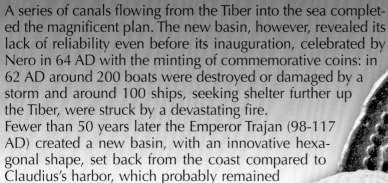

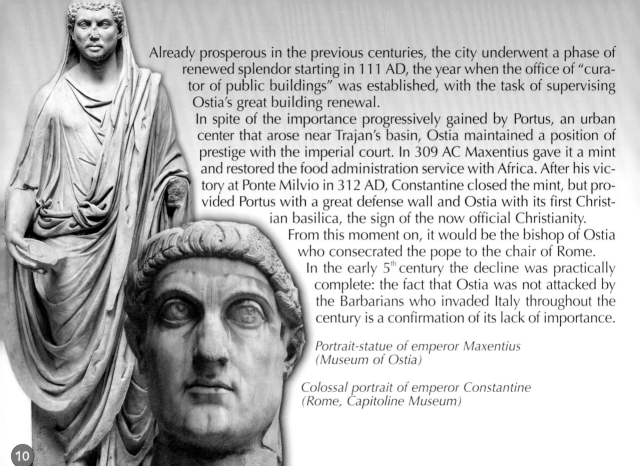

Already prosperous in the previous centuries, the city underwent a phase of renewed splendor starting in 111 AD, the year when the office of "curator of public buildings" was established, with the task of supervising Ostia's great building renewal.

In spite of the importance progressively gained by Portus, an urban center that arose near Trajan's basin, Ostia maintained a position of prestige with the imperial court. In 309 AC Maxentius gave it a mint and restored the food administration service with Africa. After his victory at Ponte Milvio in 312 AD, Constantine closed the mint, but provided Portus with a great defense wall and Ostia with its first Christian basilica, the sign of the now official Christianity.

From this moment on, it would be the bishop of Ostia who consecrated the pope to the chair of Rome.

In the early 5th century the decline was practically complete: the fact that Ostia was not attacked by the Barbarians who invaded Italy throughout the century is a confirmation of its lack of importance.

Portrait-statue of emperor Maxentius
(Museum of Ostia)

Colossal portrait of emperor Constantine
(Rome, Capitoline Museum)

It was the Saracen incursions of the 9th century AD that made the few remaining inhabitants abandon the area definitively and settle to the east of the city, where the center of Gregoriopolis rose, named after Pope Gregory IV (827-844). In fact, it was this Pope who had a wall built around the village that had already sprung up at least as far back as the 7th century, around the basilica dedicated to St. Aurea, erected in the 5th century over the tomb of the Christian martyr who fell victim, together with St. Cyriacus, to the persecutions of 269 AD.

The round fortified tower and the castle, which are still visible today, were erected by Pope Martin V first, and Julius II later, who wanted to return to Ostia its original military control role at the mouth of the Tiber.

The castle of Julius II

URBAN AND SOCIAL DEVELOPMENT

The frequentation of the area of the *castrum* in a period prior to the 4th century BC seems to be confirmed by the road system of the city of Ostia: the *cardo maximus* (the main street running north-south in Roman settlements) is laid out on a slant, probably following a pre-existing path, the so-called *Via Laurentina*, which arrived as far as the mouth of the Tiber.

In the same way, the *decumanus maximus* (the main street running east-west) seems to follow a path parallel to the river, which connected Rome with the salt beds of the river mouth. At the time of the foundation of the *castrum* the east-west layout was adjusted and it was straightened: thus was created the *Via Ostiensis*, the main road connecting Ostia with Rome which, continuing along a similar layout inside the *castrum*, formed the main street axis inside the city.

View of the Decumanus;
in the background the medieval well.

It is important to remember that Ostia originally stood near the river (which in ancient times ran parallel to the city, along the northern side) and the coastline, which was situated about 200 meters to the southwest of the walls, set back about 3 km from today's position.

It was a flooding of the Tiber in 1557 that changed its course, moving the riverbed further down.

The harbor structures were probably situated in the section to the east of the *castrum*, between it and the oxbow: for this reason, this area of the city, as far as the *Via Ostiensis*, was decreed a public area between 150 and 80 BC by *praetor*

Sample of a marble corynthian capital

Caninius, and set to be used for the structures supporting the harbor activity, the barracks for the fleet seamen, and the structures for unloading cargo.

The first fortified citadel measured 194x125.70 m, with an area of about 2.5 hectares, divided into 4 parts by the *cardo* and the *decumanus*, which crossed at the center, as was the custom in Roman settlements. Great heavy walls constructed of tuff from Fidene, of a thickness of 1.55 m and fitted with four gates, formed the defense system.

But already in the 3rd century BC, some houses were built to the east of the walls, and progressively a series of shops were set up along the eastern section of the walls, along Via dei Molini.

Between the end of the 2nd century BC and the start of the following century, a large sacred area related to the cult of Hercules developed on the opposite side, near Via della Foce, outside the walls.

Detail of a brick architectural decoration

Statue of a resting athlete from the Temple of Hercules (Museum of Ostia)

14

In 80 BC the dictator Sulla had a new defense wall built, comprising the more recently developed areas as well. With a perimeter of 1,756 m, it enclosed an area of 69 hectares, about 30 times the size of the *castrum* of the 4th century BC, originally divided into *regiones*, not corresponding to the 5 current ones, which are the result of modern conventions.

The three gates (renamed in modern times Romana, Laurentina, and Marina) were flanked by large quadrangular towers, while smaller round towers were situated along the south side; on the north side a direct connection with the port was maintained, by not building continuous walls, but only a square tower.

The building of new *horrea* (warehouses) near the Porta Romana and numerous *domus* homes – the residences of the wealthy class, laid out around an atrium or a peristyle, and generally intended for a single family – along the southern section of the *cardo*, in the area to the west of the *castrum*, and on Via della Fortuna Annonaria, bears witness to the economic prosperity of the city during this phase.

In the early imperial age (first half of the 1st century AD) the city's stateliness grew with the great Augustean and Tiberian building projects: the theater and the Piazzale delle Corporazioni (Square of the Guilds) were, in fact, the work of the first Roman emperor, while Tiberius ordered the creation of the colony's Forum and, probably, the construction of a first aqueduct. Thus rose some of the numerous thermal bath facilities that characterized the architectural development of Ostia throughout the city's lifetime.

The construction of the new port of Claudius further accentuated its commercial importance, and other warehouses were built: the *Horrea* of Hortensius and the Great *Horrea*.

The resulting population growth brought a radical change in the private building sector;

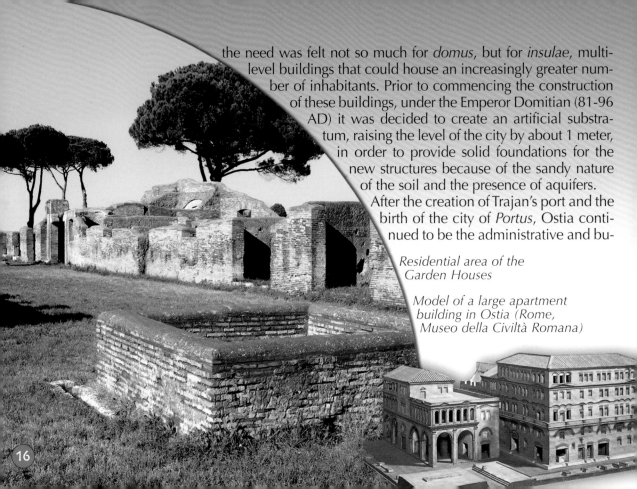

the need was felt not so much for *domus*, but for *insulae*, multi-level buildings that could house an increasingly greater number of inhabitants. Prior to commencing the construction of these buildings, under the Emperor Domitian (81-96 AD) it was decided to create an artificial substratum, raising the level of the city by about 1 meter, in order to provide solid foundations for the new structures because of the sandy nature of the soil and the presence of aquifers.

After the creation of Trajan's port and the birth of the city of *Portus*, Ostia continued to be the administrative and bu-

Residential area of the Garden Houses

Model of a large apartment building in Ostia (Rome, Museo della Civiltà Romana)

siness center of the entire complex, and new warehouses and other residences were built during this phase. Under Hadrian (117-138 AD) the new *Capitolium* was even built in the Forum, and three different projects involved the quarter to the north of the main square (large warehouses), the 2nd region (Baths of Neptune, Firemen's Barracks), and the southeastern area of the city, where the innovative Garden Houses, a luxury residential area, were built. The leitmotif of all of Hadrian's works is the use of brick, with its varied colors often exploited for aesthetic purposes.

Antoninus Pius (138-161 AD) completed and continued the projects of his predecessor, giving the city its main baths complex also: the Baths of the Forum; he was followed in this by Commodus (180-192 AD), during whose reign Ostia was even called *Colonia Felix Commodiana*. The Antonine Age was thus the moment of greatest development of the city, which by then boasted around 50,000

Fish-bone brickwork decoration from the Baths of Neptune

17

inhabitants, only a small part of whom were members of the old city aristocracy and most of whom were *homines novi*, new inhabitants belonging to families connected with trade, often the descendents of freedmen.

During the Severian Age (late 2nd-early 3rd century AD) much restoration work was done and there was a great focus on trade: the *Via Severiana* was built, running along the coast to connect Ostia and Portus with Terracina down south, and an *emporium* at the seaport. Starting in the mid-3rd century AD, signs started to be seen of a progressive decline, which led to the abandonment of numerous public buildings and some of the internal quarters. The attention of the little restoration work that was done was concentrated mainly on the service structures, and the first centers of Christian worship were created, even if Ostia, up until the end of the 4th century AD, remained a small *enclave* of pagan traditionalism. In fact, the signs of a fleeting comeback can be seen in some richly decorated *domus* belonging to merchants working in Portus and belonging to the Roman senatorial aristocracy, who were of pagan tradition.

In the 5th century AD, the decline seemed by then definitive, even if, for example, the area near Porta Marina continued to be used until the end of the century, probably by virtue of the fact that the *Via Severiana* happened to pass through it.

NECROPOLIS OF PORTA ROMANA

On entering the archaeological area, we walk along the last suburban section of the *Via Ostiensis*, still paved with blocks of basalt.

Lined up along this street are numerous sepulchral buildings which, according to very ancient laws, could not be erected *intra moenia* (inside the city walls) and were generally arranged along the main access roads to the city centers. A similar necropolis, albeit less developed and used for citizens of a lower social level, was also situated near the Porta Laurentina. Between the *Via Ostiensis* and the Via dei Sepolcri, to the south, the **necropolis of Porta Romana** was used from the 2nd century BC until the 3rd-4th century AD by the wealthy class and functionaries of the colony. It occupied only the southern part of the street, since the northern side was dedicated to harbor activities.

Necropolis of Porta Romana, tomb with columbarium

The oldest tombs (no longer visible, because they were replaced by later ones) could be dated to the 2nd century BC: they consisted of simple structures that held the urn with the ashes of the deceased (*olla*) and small accompanying objects, such as relief carvings in bone or terracotta.

Starting in the 1st century BC, the first funerary enclosures appeared, made of tuff blocks, in which the cremation rites were carried out and which then held the urns.

At the end of the 1st century BC, the most widespread type was that of the *columbarium*, a family tomb, sometimes including a second floor and characterized by the presence of numerous niches along the walls, which held the funeral urns.

Only later, toward the early 2nd century AD, the niches were replaced in some cases by

Necropolis of Porta Romana,
detail of the Tomb of the Little Arches

Decorated terracotta perfume bottles
(Museum of Ostia)

arcosolia, little arches along the walls under which marble, or more often terracotta, sarcophagi containing the body of the deceased were placed according to the burial rite.

The most interesting tombs are: the **Tomb of Hermogenes**, with its funeral inscription celebrating Domitius Fabius Hermogenes, a knight and *scriba aedilium curulium* (secretary of the *edili curuli*, the high magistracy of Rome), who was an aedile in Ostia in the late 2nd century AD; the **Tomb of the Little Arches**, along Via dei Sepolcri, from the early 1st century AD, the northern face of which still has the original polychrome architectural-style decoration.

Just beyond are the **"Colombari Gemelli"**, two tombs built in the 1st century AD, identical in plan and size, which shared a common area for the cremation pyre (*ustrinum*).

While the tomb to the east was used for a number of families, the western one belonged exclusively to the members of the *gens Cacia* and the *liberti* (freedmen) of this family.

Necropolis of Porta Romana, funerary inscription of Domitius Fabius Hermogenes

PORTA ROMANA AND DECUMANUS MAXIMUS

On the *Via Ostiensis* beyond the necropolis, stands the **Porta Romana** (Roman Gate), inserted in the walls built by Sulla in around 80 BC.

This is, in fact, the traditionally accepted date; only recently a new interpretation was proposed, setting the date of the start of construction of the walls at 63 BC, during the year of the consulate of Cicero, who must thus be credited as the promoter of the initiative.

This gate was the monumental entrance to the city for those arriving directly from Rome.

Since it was the main, and the most representative access, the gate was about 5 m wide, slightly recessed into the walls, and the central passage arch was flanked by two square-plan towers built of tuff blocks. On the attic of the entrance barrel-vault there was the inscription celebrating the original construction and the restoration, carried out in the 1st century AD,

Fragments of the marble facing of Porta Romana

Porta Romana, reconstruction

first bath buildings of the Imperial Age (first half of the 2nd century AD), known today as the **Baths of the *Cisiarii*** (Drivers). The name comes from the light mule-drawn gigs *(cisia)* depicted in one of the floor mosaics.

These were probably the private baths of the guild of the cabdrivers, who transported passengers swiftly between the city, the suburbs, and the port.

The following stretch of the Decumanus is flanked by the **porticoes** called **of the Sloping Roof** and **of Neptune**, both dating from the age of Hadrian. The former offered with its roof about 90 m of protection in front of the shops and houses and over the pedestrian walkway; the latter, two storeys high, must have held shops, at street level, and, on the upper level, rented apartments which were reached by means of independent staircases.

The so-called Republican Warehouses

Baths of the Drivers

25

BATHS OF NEPTUNE

Behind the Portico of Neptune stretched one of the largest bath complexes in Ostia: the **Baths of Neptune,** which were part of the great building renovation project begun by Hadrian and completed by Antoninus Pius in the mid-2nd century AD.

From the *solarium* of the baths, which is reached by means of a staircase, it is possible to admire the entire complex. The main entrance is on the eastern side, flanked by a *latrina* (public toilet) and the *apodyteria* (dressing rooms).

Baths of Neptune,
mosaic floor decoration

Portrait of the emperor Antoninus Pius
(Rome, Antiquarium of Palatine)

Baths of Neptune,
reconstruction of the
Frigidarium

From here there was a direct access to the large hall, the floor decoration of which has given the name to the whole complex: the fine black and white mosaic shows Neptune pulled along on his quadriga by hippocamps (fantasy animals with the head of a horse and body of a fish) and surrounded by a marine retinue of Cupids riding dolphins, Nereids, and Tritons. To the south was a room decorated with a representation of Neptune's bride, Amphitrite, on a hippocamp, accompanied by Tritons; to the north was the entrance to the large *frigidarium*, with basins at the sides for the cold baths and, in the center, a mosaic showing Scylla, a mythological sea monster. These were followed by two *tepidaria* (with basins for warm water) and, lastly, the *calidaria* for hot baths.

The heating system consisted of a series of underground wood-burning furnaces (*praefurnia*, situated along the building's perimeter), which produced hot air which was then sent into the *tubuli* running around the walls or in the

Detail of the Baths of Neptune's mosaic

Baths of Neptune, the palaestra

hollow spaces underneath the floors of the heated rooms thanks to small brick columns *(suspensurae)*. The western part of the complex was, instead, occupied by a palaestra, surrounded by rooms for resting and massages.

Although one of the most monumental, this was only one of the approximately 20 bath establishments existing in Ostia, which served to meet the needs not only of the residents, whose houses were almost totally lacking in bathroom facil-ities, but also those of the foreign seamen and merchants who would pass through Ostia.

The functioning of these facilities was made possible thanks to the relatively easy water supply that marked the city since its foundation. In an early phase, it was possible to use rainwater and the underlying aquifers, through the use of hydraulic wheels; in the Julio-Claudian age, an aqueduct was built that supplied a cistern situated underneath the gymnasium of the Baths of Neptune. A second aqueduct, built under Vespasian in the late 1st century AD, supplied water to another cistern situated near Porta Romana, just outside the walls. A network of underground lead pipes (*fistulae*) (which can be seen today through a grate near the Baths of Neptune) completed the system, bringing water to the numerous fountains punctuating the city streets, to the commercial establishments, and to the public buildings.

Caupona of Fortunatus, mosaic with cup and inscription

BARRACKS OF THE VIGILES (FIREMEN)

On the corner of Via della Fontana and the Decumanus, turning right immediately after the Baths of Neptune, is the so-called *caupona* (tavern) of Fortunatus: in reality this was a *taberna vinaria*, a sort of tavern for quick meals (a *caupona*, on the other hand, also offered lodgings).

The floor mosaic, showing a cup, still has its ancient inscription: "Fortunatus says: Since you are thirsty, drink wine from the cup!"

Along the left-hand side of Via della Fontana, are the **Insula of the Child Hercules** and the **Insula of the Painted Ceiling**, examples of the private buildings in Ostia reserved for the middle class during Hadrian's rule.

On the right side is a well-preserved fountain that gives the street its name: it is of the trunk-shaped type, very common in Ostia and ideal for keeping water cool and meeting the day-to-day needs of the population. From the Via della Fontana we reach Via della Palestra and the **Barracks of the Vigiles** for the firefighters guarding the warehouses and granaries of Ostia, which were easily subject to fires. Organized in a military manner, the cohort of the Firefighters also watched over the harbor activity and maintained law and order in the city at night.

Barracks of the Vigiles: the Caesareum's mosaic floor with scenes of a sacrifice

The Emperor Claudius had already stationed a firefighting brigade in Ostia, detached from the city garrisons, but it was Hadrian, in 137 AD, who opened the two-story complex that can still be seen today. Here there were 400 men on duty, who lived in the rooms lining a spacious central courtyard surrounded by a pillared arcade. On the east side was the entrance while, at the center of the west side, there was the *Caesareum,* a room dedicated to the cult of the imperial family, to which all military orders were particularly devoted.

In fact, by his very definition, the Emperor was the maximum authority in the military sector, as the sole holder of the *imperium*, the command of the army. Along the east side there were two *tabernae* (built later) and a latrine with an altar dedicated to Fortune, as well as two large basins for the ablutions of the soldiers, who carried out their drills in the courtyard. The equipment of the firemen consisted of axes, scythes, and pickaxes for demolitions, while we know from literary sources that, to put out the fire, they used blankets soaked in vinegar, in addition to pumped water.

Behind the Barracks, along the street named for it, there was a **Fullonica***, perhaps the largest of the four that have been discovered up to now in Ostia. The shop operated as both a laundry and a dye works for treating used garments and raw cloth to be transformed into fabrics.

Behind the three large vats that occupy the part facing the street, there are the little rooms holding the *dolia*, the terracotta containers used to press the material. Continuing along the Decumanus we reach, immediately to the east of the theater, the so-called **Christian Oratory**, a room with apse dating from the late 4th-early 5th century AD, to which, according to tradition, the body of St. Cyriacus, victim of the persecutions of 269 AD, had been transferred.

Near the oratory, but along the southern side of the Decumanus, extends one of the oldest warehouse complexes currently visible in Ostia: the **Horrea of Hortensius**, built in the 1st century AD, but used up until the 4th century AD.

Barracks of the Vigiles, reconstruction of the central courtyard

THEATER

Built at the end of the 1st century BC, the theater of Ostia is a splendid example of the propaganda initiatives of the Emperor Augustus. A place for social gathering as well as entertainment, the building also enriched the urban decor, a sign of the imperial benevolence. Enlarged by Commodus and restored by Septimius Severus, it is still being used thanks to modern restoration work.

We find ourselves before a typical "Roman" theater which, unlike the "Greek" theater, is not backed up against the slope of a hill, but is built of masonry, with an external portico with concrete arches and vaults, capable of supporting the internal structure and in which there are *tabernae,* staircases, and cisterns.

The main entrance, on the Decumanus, flanked in the 3rd century by two monumental arches dedicated to Caracalla, consisted of a corridor whose vault was decorated in stucco with a

*Theater: cavea, orchestra and
the remains of the stage*

Theater, reconstruction of the external portico

motif of octagonal and round shapes, alternating with framed figural scenes. There is still one with Victory (the winged maiden) crowning Hercules, a god to whom Commodus was particularly devoted. The *cavea*, where the audience sat, has at the present time been rebuilt only for two of the three original levels, which arrived at holding up to 4,000 spectators. Important personages had reserved seats on the lower levels, closer to the stage.

At the sides of the semicircular orchestra were the *parodoi*, the performers' entrances. Behind the actual stage, with a front having small curvilinear and rectangular niches, there was a tuff wall, from Augustan times, on a small part of which can still be seen fragments of the marble architectural decoration.

It is possible to recognize the typical masks, a reproduction of those actually used (made of cloth or wood) to amplify the voice and play the female roles better, since these were played by male actors, because women were not allowed to take part in plays.

The traditional tragedies and comedies were gradually joined over time by more popular genres, such as mime and farce (a sort of parody, generally of a

Marble mask of the theater's architectural decoration

mythological subject) and, in the 4th century AD, even *tetimimi* (water games).

The water kept in the cisterns arranged along the external circuit was conveyed into the entrance corridor and sent into the *orchestra*, which was transformed into a sort of pool (*colimbreta*) by means of a marble barrier that separated it from the *cavea*.

View of Piazzale delle Corporazioni

PIAZZALE DELLE CORPORAZIONI

Behind the theater lies the great **Piazzale delle Corporazioni (Square of the Guilds)**. Originally built by Augustus and directly connected with the theater activities, used as a place for walking and resting for the spectators in the event of rain, it took on the form that is visible today between the 2nd and the 3rd century AD. It was then that it became the center of the city's economic and commercial life.

Piazzale delle Corporazioni, details of the mosaic with maritime motifs and symbols of the guilds

Behind the double arcade of columns surrounding the whole square, a series of rooms were built to house the *stationes,* i.e. the offices of the guilds *(collegia)* of shopkeepers, craftsmen, and merchants operating in Ostia. They were probably used for trade and selling activities and, generally speaking, they were a point of reference for the *negotiatores* (traders) passing through Ostia, and coming from all over the Mediterranean region.

The decorations of the floor mosaics of each of these rooms offer a significant panorama of the intensity and variety of the economic life of Ostia. In addition to the black and white mosaics forming seafaring and commercial designs (the Lighthouse of Ostia with cargo ships entering the harbor, the unloading of amphorae from the ships, a river with a bridge of boats), there are also the symbols of several guilds of workers, such as the *stuppatores restiones* (tow and

The elephant, symbol of the city of Sabratha, in northern Africa

rope merchants) or the *corpus pellionum* (tanners), and of ship owners *(navicularii)*.

In other cases there is the city of origin of the various shopkeepers: Sabratha, symbolized by an elephant, Alexandria, Carthage, Narbonne, Cagliari, Porto Torres.

At the center of the square there is a temple, perhaps dedicated to Ceres, the goddess of agriculture, connected with goddesses of good harvests and commercial fortune; while the portico was decorated with statues depicting the most important citizens of the colony.

MITHRAEUM OF THE SEVEN SPHERES

I mmediately to the west of the theater is the **House of Apuleius**, so called because of the finding of a lead *fistula* bearing the name of a certain *P. Apuleius*.

Built during the reign of Trajan, it is one of the last examples in Ostia of the rich *domus* of Republican tradition. The complex has an unusual "L" shape, determined by the need to fit into an area already occupied by earlier buildings. It develops around an atrium with a central basin, elements that recall the houses in Pompeii, but surrounded by columns, a feature that would be characteristic of the private buildings of a later age.

The rooms preserved in the west sector (some of which equipped with heating systems, consisting of pipes running along the walls) still show traces of remodelings done up until the 3rd century AD: the original inlaid marble floors *(opus sectile)* were replaced with black and white mosaics depicting Gorgons, Nereids, Satyrs and Maenads, and wrestlers.

From the House of Apuleius we arrive at the **Mithraeum of the Seven Spheres**, one of the approximately 20 mithraea found up to now in Ostia. Originally a Persian god, Mithra was the sun god, the god of light, and represented the victory of good over evil. His cult, steeped in mystery and connected with the astrological symbolism of the Eastern world, spread to the West and to Italy toward the end of the 1st century AD, mainly by way of soldiers and merchants coming from the eastern regions of the Empire, and it reached its peak in Ostia between the 2nd and 3rd century AD.

The places of worship were usually in small, dark, isolated or underground chambers, which reproduced the cave where Mithra himself, generated from rock, had seen the light of Victory.

The initiation rites, in which a small number of faithful took part, followed a complex cosmic symbolism and a rigid hierarchy, as did the sacrifices, which ended with the killing of a bull, the symbol of darkness and matter.

And this is precisely the episode depicted on the relief found at the back of the mithraeum (it is actually a plaster cast of the original, which is kept in the Vatican Museum).

There were seven degrees of elevation that the initiates could go through, represented here by the seven semicircles still visible on the mosaic floor, a metaphor of the seven spheres of the planets. And precisely the seven planets are represented on the sides of the *praesepia* (the side benches on which the faithful would recline during the sacrifices), while the top surfaces show the seven signs of the zodiac.

South of the Mythraeum is the area of the **Four Little Temples**, built by P. Lucilius Gamala, a magistrate of Ostia and member of one of the most prominent families during the 1st century BC; they were dedicated to Venus, Fortune, Ceres, and Hope, goddesses of good omen, very probably the subject of devotion especially by seamen, considering the closeness of the sacred area to the river landing point.

On the south side of the Decumanus, along the Via degli Augustali, stands the **Tempio**

Mithraeum of the Seven Spheres, reconstruction

Collegiale (Guild Temple), erected toward the end of the 2nd century AD by the rich guild of the *Fabri Tignuarii* (builders), probably in honor of the deified Emperor Pertinax (193 AD), who had perhaps enacted measures that benefited the trade associations.

HALL OF THE AUGUSTALES, FULLONICAE

On the opposite side of the street is the **Hall of the Augustales**, the political-religious guild reserved for freedmen, who were in charge of the cult of the imperial household: a statue depicting one of the members made it possible to identify the complex.

The guild, made up of six members (at least in an early phase), with the passing of time became one of the most thriving in Ostia, a powerful instrument of social promotion for the wealthier freedmen.

The high economic level achieved by the guild is also reflected in the rich decorations of the rooms: around an arcaded courtyard are arranged rooms with painted walls and lovely polychrome mosaic floors, and a central room with an apse, decorated with marble slabs.

The Hall of the Augustales

It was here that the statues of the emperors were probably situated; those on display now are plaster casts of the originals kept in the Musem of Ostia, and it was here that the statue of the emperor Maxentius (306-312 AD) dressed in the robes of the *pontifex maximus*, the high priest, was found.

South of the building can be seen another of the numerous **fullonicae** of Ostia, it, too, equipped with vats for the *saltus fullonicus*, the pressing with the bare feet of the cloth being dyed.

To obtain the desired color, they were rubbed and mixed in ammonia-base liquids, after washing them, passing them from the larger vats to the smaller ones. Among the most requested colors was red, used in particular for the edges of the senators' togas and obtained by diluting the extract of a mollusc with urine. The result was splendidly colored but offensive smelling, as mentioned by some ancient writers.

After the *fullonica*, we take the Via della Fortuna Annonaria, which owes its name to a nearby aristocratic house: the **Domus of the Fortuna Annonaria** which, rebuilt in the 4th century AD by radically modifying a previous residence, is an example of an aristocratic house of the late imperial age, when the taste for the Pompeiian type comfortable residences came back into style. The center of the complex is a spacious internal garden with a portico along the sides and a fountain in the middle, onto which all the rooms of the house face, decorated with polychrome marbles and figural mosaics.

Worthy of note is the nymphaeum on the west side, separated by an arched passageway.

The sculptural decoration was also rich, featuring numerous representations of goddesses and personifications connected with trade and the fertility of the fields, a detail that has led to the theory that the house belonged to a food administration magistrate.

Taking the Semita dei Cippi (Tombstone Alley) toward the Decumanus, we go by the **"Insula dell'Invidioso"** (of the Envious One), so called after an inscription preserved in the *taberna* at the southwestern corner, built in the mid-2nd

Domus of the Fortuna Annonaria, inside garden with portico

HOUSE OF DIANA

G oing along Via dei Molini, we reach the crossing with Via di Diana; from here we arrive at the most central area of ancient Ostia: the quarter around the Forum, where most of the commercial activities were concentrated; these were certainly the most crowded streets of the city.

For this reason, at the sides of the Via di Diana, well paved and complete with sidewalk, there are numerous *insulae* (apartment buildings), built in around the mid-2nd century AD.

Consisting of several floors, they were made up of rented apartments, housing families of a more modest level than the *domus*, which were reserved for the aristocratic classes.

The *insula* generally had an elegant balconied façade *(moeniana)* of brick, and must have risen for three or four floors, while the rooms on the ground floor held shops and *tabernae*, over which there was a **floor** with the apartment of the shop's caretaker or owner.

A law dictated that the maximum total height could be 18-20 m; a complex system of staircases led to the various levels; those of the lower floors were reserved for the middle-class families, while the higher floors were for the less well-to-do and the servants.

The **House of Diana**, built around a central courtyard, which provided air and light to the entire complex, still preserves part of the façade up to the 2nd-floor balcony, and probably also housed a sort of inn for travelers, served by a common latrine.

A fountain in the internal courtyard was decorated with a relief showing Diana, goddess of the hunt.

The presence of a small mithraeum, created in two rooms on the north side, also provides indications as to the heterogeneous nature of the guests and the vivacity of the cultural and social life of the city in the 2nd century AD.

In the **"Piazzetta dei Lari"**, opposite the House of Diana, are preserved the altar and the fountain dedicated to the *Lares Compitales,* the protectors of the quarter. A short distance ahead, opposite the *Thermopolium*, is the **Caseggiato dei Dipinti (Tenement of the Paintings)**, divided into several *insulae* for rent (in which part of the pictorial and mosaic decorations is still preserved), with a staircase leading up to a terrace, which affords a splendid view of the entire archaeological area.

Behind this is the **Caseggiato dei Doli**, which contains around 35 *dolia defossa* (large terracotta jars set into the ground) for storing solid or liquid foodstuffs (oil and wine). The average capacity of these *dolia*, as indicated on some of

1ˢᵗ century BC relief with market scene (Museum of Ostia)

them, was 40 *amphorae* (each amphora contained about 26 liters).

"CASEGGIATO" OF THE THERMOPOLIUM

On the left side of the Via di Diana is the **"Caseggiato" of the Thermopolium**, with external balconies supported by travertine brackets. On the ground floor are the three entrances to one of the numerous taverns that existed to serve the citizens of Ostia, but especially the merchants, craftsmen, laborers, and harbor workers who arrived in the city with the cargo ships. Thanks to modern restoration, it is still possible to understand the internal structure of this *popina* (the Latin name of this type of commercial enterprise), subdivided into

Thermopolium, the main room

Thermopolium, the counter and painted panel showing the food for sale

three rooms, with the main one in the center: here there was the sales counter, faced with marble slabs and equipped with two basins for washing the tableware and shelves for displaying the foods. A painting shows the foods available for the guests: eggs in brine, grapes, olives, a hot turnip; also shown are cymbals, indicating the musical accompaniment to be enjoyed during the meals.

The room to the right was perhaps the kitchen, judging by the remains of a masonry oven and the presence of a jar sunken into the floor to keep fresh food.

The outside courtyard, decorated in the center with a small fountain, was used for eating outside in the summer months.

One of the entrances still has the threshold, with the groove for sliding the wooden panels commonly used for closing commercial establishments in this type of building.

The "Caseggiato" (Tenement) of the Thermopolium, reconstruction of the façade

Forum Baths, detail of the palaestra

Public latrine near the Forum Baths

FORUM BATHS

The magnificent **Forum Baths** were erected at the southeastern end of the Forum in around the mid-2nd century AD, as ordered by M. Gavius Maximus, the prefect of the praetorium (a very high office reserved for members of the upper middle class), and were used until a very late period.

The main entrance, on the Via della Forica, led into a large *frigidarium* with basins on the sides for regenerating baths, going through passages lined with dressing rooms. An inscription on an architrave fragment found here mentions precisely the *loutron alexipo(non)*, i.e., the "bath that soothes pain".

The rooms reserved for sunbathing, sauna, and hot baths were arranged along the southern side, to exploit the sunrays as much as possible,

especially in the afternoon hours, when the baths were most frequented. Proof of the use of this bath establishment by women as well, at certain hours, as laid out by a series of laws, lies in the large quantity of hair pins found in one of the rooms of the complex.

A large palaestra to the south and a library probably completed the building. The southwest corner of the palaestra was occupied by a small temple, of which the god worshipped there is unknown.

Leaving the Baths, along the street skirting the north side is a **public latrine**, which was entered through a turnstile, of which the marks remain on the entrance threshold; inside there were twenty seats with basins and channels for water.

Between the Forum Baths and the Decumanus is the **"Caseggiato" of the Triclinia**, site of the guild of the *Fabri Tignuarii* (the builders), a guild that became very important especially during the reign of Hadrian, as a result of the great building expansion of Ostia ordered by the emperor himself.

Along the central courtyard, elegantly decorated with columns, are the rooms for the guild's banquets, which still contain the *triclinia*, from which the building takes its name, and a room reserved for the imperial cult.

Bone-made hairpins (Museum of Ostia)

THE FORVM

From the Via di Diana we reach the main square of Ostia: the Forum, the political and social center of the city.

Excavation surveys carried out in the area have shown that, at the time of the foundation of the *castrum*, there was no actual clearly marked forum square, but probably the first public buildings and main temples were, in any case, in this area (remains of some of them and of a section of the Republican *cardo maximus* can be seen in a small excavation in the northern part of the square).

Only during the Imperial Age, starting with the reign of Tiberius, the Forum acquired a real monumental nature, completed in the currently visible phase during the time of Hadrian.

The Forum Square, detail

Looking onto the square, surrounded by colonnades, were the monuments symbolizing the Roman tradition. Indeed, along the north side stands the **Capitolium**, the main temple, dedicated to the Capitoline triad (Jupiter, Juno, and Minerva), an ideal replica of the Temple of Jupiter Optimus Maximus on the Capitol, in Rome. It was built in around 120 AD entirely of brick, with marble revetment, now completely gone; on the walls of the chamber were niches, while against the back wall there was a tripartite podium for the three statues of the cult. Below the temple there were three large chambers, probably used as archives for the public documents and State treasury (*aerarium publicum*). On the opposite side of the square

Northern side of the Forum: the Capitolium

stands the **Temple of Augustus and Rome**, used for the celebration of the imperial cult.

Only a few fragments of the pediment and the cult statue of Rome dressed as an Amazon remain of the building.

It is probable that there was a tribune for orators and judges on the temple façade.

To the west of the *Capitolium*, on the north side of the Decumanus, is a square plan building, with a 6-column portico on the front, normally identified as the **Curia**, the seat of the *decuriones*, the local Senate. The small size and absence of seats for the 100 participants in the meetings have led to doubts as to the building's function, and some scholars have proposed to identify it as the seat of the *seviri Augustales*, those in charge of the imperial cult.

On the opposite side of the Decumanus is the judicial **Basilica** built, like the Curia, during Trajan's time. It consisted of a magnificent hall, originally richly decorated in marble, that still preserves some of its Corinthian columns and the judges' tribune.

ROUND TEMPLE

Next to the Basilica is the so-called **Round Temple**, the original use of which is not yet known with certainty. It has been theorized that it may be a sort of *Pantheon* (for the worship of all gods) or *Augusteum* (temple of the imperial household; indeed, numerous statues of the imperial family were found inside).

It has also been supposed, considering the great size of the chamber, that the building might have been used for holding public meetings on the occasion of exceptional circumstances, which required the presence of the entire local Senate, such as the death of the Emperor or the election of high magistrates. Built in the mid-3rd century AD by transforming the already-existing square at the front into a sacred enclosure, the temple underwent numerous restoration operations during the age of Constantine.

Erected on a high podium, it was preceded by a monumental columned entrance, which was reached by way of a monumental staircase.

Round Temple: reconstruction of the front and of the sacred enclosure

The circular chamber had niches on the walls, alternating with columns, of which only the bases remain. Two spiral staircases (one still partly preserved) led up to the dome. Across from the temple was the **House of the Lararium**, built under the reign of Hadrian.

A series of shops and workshops opened onto the inner courtyard, where a niche contained the sacred statues of the Lares (protective spirits).

We return to the Decumanus and reach a crossing with Via della Foce; here there were originally the western gate of the *castrum* and the walls dating from the 4th century BC, of which little remains.

HORREA EPAGATHIANA AND EPAPHRODITIANA

Turning right, we go along the Via Epagathiana until we reach the entrance to the Horrea Epagathiana and Epaphroditiana, a large warehouse complex, thus called on a marble slab referring to the two owners of the building, Epagathes and Epaphrodites. The Greek origin surnames seem

Horrea Epagathiana, the entrance portal

Reconstruction of the Horrea Epagathiana façade

to indicate that they were two freedmen who had become wealthy thanks to their commercial activities. The complex was thus a private commercial warehouse.

The entrance portal, done in two-color brick-work, flanked by two Corinthian columns and topped with a tympanum, was completely re-built using the original fragments.

It is a splendid example of the building techniques most used during the Antonine period, in the mid-2nd century AD.

The entrance had a double door closed with iron bars, to protect the goods kept inside, which were evidently of value.

The warehouse consisted of two stories, built around a porticoed courtyard, with niches for the statues of *Agathè Tyche* (Good Fortune) and Aphrodite. The rooms on the ground floor were used to store the goods.

The upper floor, with a loggia, was reserved for the apartments of the proprietors, and was accessible directly from the street by means of travertine staircases.

To the east of the complex was the so-called **Small Market**, another building used to store various goods, but not grain, considering the lack of insulating hollow spaces underneath the floors. Grain must have been stored in the building to the north, the **"Caseggiato" dei Misuratori del Grano (the Grain Measurers)**, at least judging by the image of a *modius* (the container and unit of measurement for grain) carved into the pediment of the entrance portal.

HOUSE OF CUPID AND PSYCHE

After the entrance to the *Horrea Epagathiana* and turning west, we visit the **Baths of Buticosus**, thus called after the name of the bath attendant whose image appears in the floor mosaic of one of the dressing rooms. This and other mosaic decorations preserved here have been attributed to the same artisan who created the splendid mosaics of the Baths of Neptune. More than an actual baths complex, it is a *balneum*, a more modest structure run by private owners.

House of Cupid and Psyche,
reconstruction of the nymphaeum

A narrow passageway leads to the **House of Cupid and Psyche**, a rich house organized around a central atrium, on the western side of which there are four rooms.

In one of these, richly decorated by polychrome marbles, was discovered the small sculpture group that gave the building its name. On the east side is the nymphaeum, with niches from which the water ran, which adorned the back part of a *viridarium* (garden) reached through a colonnaded portico.

The presence of the nymphaeum in this *domus* is an example of the adaptation for private use of a characteristic monument of the public building sector and a clear indication of the high social level of the owners of the complex, and thus of part of Ostia's population, at least up until the early 4th century AD, the time the house was built.

The decoration of the main room, to the north, with its walls and floors in *opus sectile* (colored marble tesserae) is also very rich.

Continuing westward, it is possible to visit the **Baths of Mithras**, which still hold the *noria*, i.e. the hydraulic wheel used to draw water from underground. From the mithraeum, an underground chamber of the baths turned into a place of worship, came the fragments of the cult statue, the work of a Greek artist, depicting Mithra killing the bull (the recomposed original is in the Museum).

Going back to the Via della Foce, we come to the seat of the guild of the **Mensores**, the grain measurers, whose activity is shown in the mosaic still preserved in the large hall, used for meetings: the *mensor* is shown with the *modius* and the *rutellum*, a stick used to level the grain in the *modius*; around him are the porters and an assistant, intent on counting the sacks of grain, threading beads on a string.

Cupid embracing Psyche, Roman copy from a late-Hellenistic original

"CASEGGIATO" OF SERAPIS
BATHS OF THE SEVEN SAGES
INSULA OF THE CHARIOTEERS

S outh of the Via della Foce we reach the **"Caseggiato" of Serapis** (from the period of Hadrian), which takes its name from a shrine dedicated to this Egyptian god, added later in the south-western corner of the courtyard, which encloses a small figure of Serapis in painted stucco.

The central courtyard is surrounded by rooms, probably *tabernae,* while the up-per level probably contained the apart-ments for the numerous easterners who lived in the area.

Aligned with the Caseggiato of Serapis are the **Baths of the Seven Sages**, thus called after a painting showing the Seven Greek Sages, preserved in a room that was originally a shop and later

The "Caseggiato" (Tenement) of Serapis

63

Baths of the Seven Sages, circular room of the frigidarium

Baths of the Seven Sages, painting with Venus

turned into an *apodyterium* (dressing room) for the baths. Only some of the portraits are still visible, accompanied by their names in Greek and by humorous sayings alluding to physiological functions, recalling the Latin comic theater.

Also built during the period of Hadrian, the baths were intended essentially to meet the needs of the inhabitants of the great adjacent residential complexes, but they were probably open to the public also.

The structure and the mosaic decoration of the circular room of the *frigidarium* are well preserved: on the floor is an elaborate hunting scene, while in one of the niches it is possible to see one of the few preserved examples of polychrome wall mosaics. The room with basins (a second *frigidarium*) situated on the opposite side of the complex has, on the other hand, a delicate image of Venus Anadiomenes (emerging from the waters) with cupids, in a toilette scene.

A small courtyard joins the Baths with the **Insula of the Charioteers**, the name of which derives from the pictorial depiction of two charioteers with their chariots and crowns, visible on the north wall of the corridor. The center of the residential complex, erected in around 140 AD, is the large inner courtyard with arched porticoes that are repeated for the upper floors as well (part of the third is also preserved), around which are arranged apartments for rent as living quarters or as workshops, which have produced some of the most refined examples of painting in Ostia.

Geometric decorations, hunting scenes, mythological and genre scenes fill the rooms to the west of the courtyard.

The double portico with brick pillars, arranged obliquely along the southern side to connect the tenement with the Via degli Aurighi, is very particular.

Painting with charioteer

Insula of the Charioteers, remains of the central building

Along the west side of the complex runs an interesting *via tecta* (covered and arched way), while on the eastern side there is the **Shrine of the Three Naves**, built in around the mid-2nd century AD.

Divided into a nave and two aisles by small columns and podiums, stuccoed in red, it was probably used for the rituals of some guild connected with one of the numerous eastern religions practiced in Ostia during that period.

TEMPLE OF HERCULES

Returning to the *Via della Foce* and continuing eastward, it is possible to visit the **Republican Sacred Area**, a sort of square on which stood several sacred complexes of fundamental importance for the religious life of Ostia.

The main building is the **Temple of Hercules**, erected toward the end of the 2nd century BC along the western limit of the square and facing, according to tradition, eastward.

It stands on a tall podium reached by means of a wide staircase, and was originally endowed with 6 columns on the front and 3 at the sides of the pronaos. From the temple come a marble statue base bearing a dedication to Hercules, dating from the 2nd century BC and an altar from the 4th century AD, demonstrating that the cult continued throughout the entire imperial age. The cast of a statue of a resting athlete (the original is in the Museum) standing in the pronaos was intended to be a heroic, idealized portrait of Cartilius Poplicola, several times a magistrate of the colony.

Hercules was venerated here as the protector of trade, but also as an oracular god, to whom mainly the fleet commanders requested omens before setting sail. In fact, the position of the temple is particular, outside of the walls and in the direction of the sea; in this area, a votive relief was also found, which shows the miraculous catching of a statue of the god in a fishing net, and the reading of the oracles.

Instead, the so-called **Tetrastyle Temple**, erected at the same time along the north side of the

Temple of Hercules, reconstruction

square, and also connected with the Tiber, must have been dedicated to Aesculapius; this god had, in Rome, his main temple on the Isola Tiberina.

On the other hand, the name of the deity venerated in the so-called **Temple of the Round Altar**, built along the south side, is unknown. In front of it were found a circular altar decorated with cupids, and numerous statue bases brought to Rome from Greece probably during the reign of Sulla (1st century BC) and placed here as votive offerings.

Also objects of veneration were the four altars (the oldest of which dating from around 250 BC) arranged in an enclosure along the east side of the square. Continuing this route, we reach the crossing of the Via della Foce with the Decumanus, leading respectively to the Tiber and to the sea.

On the left we find the **Tabernae (Stalls) of the Fishmongers**, with a tank to keep the fish alive, a selling table, a counter for cooking the fish, and a floor mosaic showing a dolphin biting into an octopus. Behind these is the *Macellum*, the meat market, used from the 1st century BC to the 5th century AD, with selling counters arranged along the west side of a courtyard with a marble pavement and fountain in the center.

Taberna of the Fishmonger near the Macellum

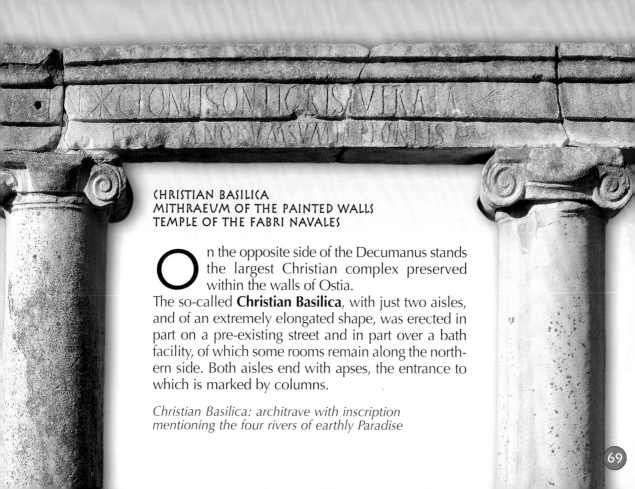

CHRISTIAN BASILICA
MITHRAEUM OF THE PAINTED WALLS
TEMPLE OF THE FABRI NAVALES

On the opposite side of the Decumanus stands the largest Christian complex preserved within the walls of Ostia.

The so-called **Christian Basilica**, with just two aisles, and of an extremely elongated shape, was erected in part on a pre-existing street and in part over a bath facility, of which some rooms remain along the northern side. Both aisles end with apses, the entrance to which is marked by columns.

Christian Basilica: architrave with inscription mentioning the four rivers of earthly Paradise

On the architrave entering the left-hand room are mentioned the four rivers of earthly Paradise: Geon, Phison, Tigris, and Euphrates, and for this reason it was long believed that the building was a baptistery. The most accredited hypothesis today is that it was a place of worship for some martyr or a school for catechumens, or even the seat of a sect of heretics.

Behind the Basilica is the **Mithraeum of the Painted Walls**, created in the mid-2nd century AD inside a Republican age house; the podiums for the worshippers, an altar with relief decorations, and part of the pictorial decorations on the walls are still preserved.

They refer to the various degrees of initiation the followers of Mithra had to pass: still visible are the *Nymphus,* dressed as a woman, the *Miles,* running with a lowered rod, and the *Heliodromus*, with a raised torch.

Alongside the Christian complex there are a series of structures belonging to a **temple** and a porticoed courtyard, in which the place of worship of the **Fabri Navales,** the shipwrights, has been recognized on the basis of an inscription found on the base of a statue, with a dedication to their protector. The guild also handled the maintenance and supervision of the merchant fleet. Only the walls of the podium remain of the temple, erected at the end of the 2nd century AD; it was originally tetrastyle (with 4 columns on the front), and was reached by means of a staircase, while a portico surrounded the courtyard in front of the sacred building.

SCHOLA OF TRAJAN

Facing the temple of the *Fabri Navales,* and directly related to it, is the **Schola of Trajan,** thus called after the statue of the Emperor Trajan found here and now in the Museum. Built in the mid-2nd century AD on an area formerly occupied by an Augustan *domus*, the Schola was probably the headquarters of the rich guild of the *Fabri Navales.*

Four Corinthian columns marked the monumental street entrance and led into an exedra with a marble floor and two large fountain

Temple of the Fabri Navales: reconstruction of the front and of the colonnaded portico

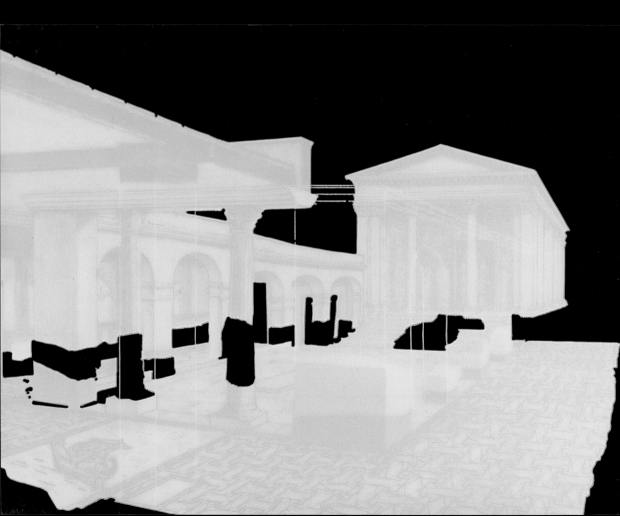

Insula of the Muses, pictorial wall decoration of the triclinium

niches; this led into the vast central courtyard, at the back of which was the room with apse and twisted columns, used for social banquets, on the occasion of the launching of a new ship or the arrival of an important guest.
The floor was decorated with a mosaic of animals and winged geniuses set into a pattern of spiraling plants, simpler in the bands along the walls, which were to be hidden by the triclinia. Next to the central room are smaller rooms and

a three-seat latrine. We go back once again to the Decumanus and, turning right onto Via degli Aurighi and then left onto Via delle Volte Dipinte, we reach two residential buildings, one across from the other: the **Insula of the Muses** and the **Insula of the Painted Vaults**. The first of the two is an aristocratic residence with a central porticoed courtyard, which was built when the quarter was fixed up on Hadrian's order, who created

one of the most beautiful residential areas of the whole city here.

It is, in reality, a two-story *domus*, reserved for a single high-class family only, as evidenced by the refined paintings showing Apollo and the nine Muses, with Dionysian scenes and showy architecture. On the opposite side of the street is the **Insula of the Painted Vaults**, with a much simpler plan, without an inner central courtyard, but with rooms arranged along two sides of a corridor. The pictorial decoration, which shows five different reworking phases, features Dionysian scenes with dancers, and genre scenes with cupids and pygmies.

The state of preservation of the paintings that decorated the vaulted ceilings of the rooms, with geometric patterns and bright colors, is remarkable. Slightly more to the south is the **Domus of the Dioscuri**, with lovely polychrome floor mosaics dating from the 4th century AD, and the contemporary **Domus of the Nymphaeum**, with complex interior architectural solutions.

But the most interesting and particular complex of this residential area are the **Garden Houses**. At the center of a large trapezoidal courtyard laid out like a garden and endowed with six fountains, stand two rectangular blocks, each of which held four two-floor apartments, all of the same shape and size.

Isolated from the street thanks to the garden and lacking *taberna*e, these apartments were a guarantee of functionality and privacy.

PORTA MARINA, SYNAGOGUE

Taking the Decumanus southward, we reach the **Porta Marina**, the third gate of Sulla's wall, partly incorporated into the Hadrianic *tabernae* built over it.

Closer to the sea and thus more open to attacks, the gate has some structural particularities: the masonry is reinforced with tuff blocks placed at right angles, and the two square towers at the sides protrude from the line of the wall itself, for greater defense.

The area immediately outside of the Porta Marina was originally used as a necropolis, and only starting in the 1st century AD were the first public buildings erected there. In the 3rd century AD the *Via Severiana* was built, to connect Terracina, Ostia and Portus, guaranteeing the quarter's vitality at least until the 4th century AD.

Just outside of the Gate we find, on the left, the so-called **Forum of Porta Marina**, a large porticoed courtyard, the function of which has not yet been clarified: a parking place for carts passing through, or an open-air place of worship are the theories put forward so far. Connected to the "Forum" is the **Sanctuary of the Bona Dea** (protectress of fertility), the object of a mystery cult for women only.

Stretch of the Decumanus
towards Porta Marina

The actual temple, hidden by a closed courtyard, was reached through a narrow passageway.

After passing the **Domus Fulminata** (House Struck by Lightning), thus called in remembrance of a lightning bolt, we see, at the corner of the street with the same name, the **Tomb of Cartilius Poplicola**, erected at the end of the 1st century BC and incorporated only during the reign of Hadrian into the Loggia of Cartilius, a covered parking area.

The Domus Fulminata, end of the 1st century AD

The Domus Fulminata, mosaic representing Helios

The monumental tomb is made of tuff, covered with travertine and marble; on the front can be read the dedicatory inscription, with a description of the brilliant career of this important citizen of Ostia, who stood out also as defender of the city in some naval conflict, an event to which the frieze depicting a war, decorating the upper part of the tomb, seems to refer.

At the end of Via di Cartilio is the complex of the **Baths of Porta Marina** (or **of Marciana**, after the name of Emperor Trajan's sister, whose colossal portrait was found in the building).

Begun by Trajan, the baths underwent various remodelings, up to the period of Theodoric (493-526 AD), bearing witness to the long life and vitality of the quarter.

Baths of Porta Marina or of Marciana, the Frigidarium's apsis

The floor mosaics still show scenes of award-winning athletes, fish subjects, and sea scenes. To the east of the baths is the **Synagogue**, whose establishment, very ancient, dates back to about the mid-1st century AD.

Scholars believe that, already at that time, a Jewish community had sprung up in Ostia, perhaps thanks to the kindliness of the imperial household. The temple was, in any case, rebuilt in the 4th century.

Through a portico and a passageway flanked by curtain walls, we arrive in the hall of worship, with the shrine of the Torah, where the Laws were kept, and shelves decorated in relief with the *menorah*

Baths of Porta Marina: details of the mosaic floors with athletes and fish motifs

(the seven-branched candelabrum), the *lulav* with the *etrog* (a sheaf of three plant species together with a citron), and the *shofar* (ram's horn).

A second room to the south was probably used for meetings.

In one of the side rooms there were an oven for baking the unleavened bread and a counter for kneading the bread dough, while the well for the ritual ablutions was in the entrance. The Decumanus ends in front of the colonnaded entrance to a splendid late-antique *domus*.

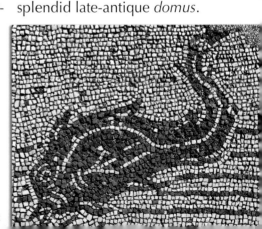

Completely transformed in the 4th century AD, the structure was endowed with a rich floor and wall decoration in *opus sectile* (polychrome marble tesserae), showing various subjects, including a bearded figure identified as a "blessing Christ" or a "philosopher".
On the western side of the building is a section of the dam built to protect this suburban area from the high tides.

The Synagogue

Wall decoration in polychrome marble of a late-antique domus

Text by the **Soprintendenza Archeologica of Ostia**
with updating revision by **E. Interdonato** - University of Rome "La Sapienza"
Drawings and reconstructions: Vision s.r.l.
Graphic project and layout: Federico Schneider
Photographs by Vision s.r.l., Spazio Visivo, Corbis, Contrasto, Scala.

VISION
ROMA
PAST & PRESENT

1st Edition 1981
New edition 2009
Copyright © 2009 VISION s.r.l.

VISION s.r.l. - Via Livorno 20 - 00162 Rome (Italy) - Tel/Fax (39) 0644292688
E-mail: info@visionpubl.com

ISBN: 978-88-8162-266-5

Printed in Italy by Tipolitographica CS - Padova